WILLIAM KOTZWINKLE

ILLUSTRATED BY

JOE SERVELLO

SEDUCTION IN BERLIN

G. P. PUTNAM'S SONS   NEW YORK

G. P. PUTNAM'S SONS
Publishers Since 1838
200 Madison Avenue
New York, NY 10016

Library of Congress Cataloging in Publication Data

Kotzwinkle, William.
    Seduction in Berlin.

    I. Title.
PS3561 085S4   1985   811'.54   84-13441
ISBN 0-399-12955-3

PRINTED IN THE UNITED STATES OF AMERICA
1   2   3   4   5   6   7   8   9   10

SEDUCTION IN BERLIN

The dancers move past you through the smoke—
    no equal have they in Berlin,
their exquisite movements able to evoke
    all that you have been
    and what you must become
    to the beating of the drum.

Upon the shining floor, reflected in its glass
their flowing lines define our dream.
But we must see them as they are,
which is to say, against a star
whose light, splintered and refracted
causes their dance to be enacted
by many glittering reflections cast
into other dimensions, future and past.

This is the dance seen any night in Berlin.
Please—you are invited in.

"Of all times the present is most difficult
    to understand . . ."
The Baron said this as he entered.
". . . we have no perspective on the minute hand
    nor on the hour, day, or year.
Only a decade will do to make it clear."

The Waiter, overhearing, said softly,
"Let the dancers assist you."

"Eh?" The Baron twisted toward him impatiently,
wishing to be seated immediately,
before a minute passed in waiting,
for he despised hesitating of any sort.

The party swept forward, the Baron,
the Baroness and a second escort,
her lover, a young man she'd helped to discover.

"Night with its attendant modes," said the Waiter,
    seating them,
then withdrawing again to the door
welcoming another aide to the Chancellor.

So the evening's guests arrive
some dead, some alive.
Is the dance floor transcendental?
Or merely ornamental?

Sad images and bright gather there.
The deceased Foreign Minister rises from his chair,
    bows to the Baroness
    who turns her head
    but she cannot see the dead,
    only feels a memory stir
as the dancers glide on past her
and then the memory is gone,
    a black swan
    in a dark pool.

I am such a fool . . .

She looks at her young lover,
whom the Baron too must inevitably discover.
. . . Oh, but I cannot face loneliness tonight.
Let it be banished until daylight.

"Each thing has its place,"
the Baron was saying,
"And here you will surely see a face
you have seen before . . ."

He spoke to their young guest, a decorator
who knew the club better than the Baron ever could,
and understood
the meaning of its muted light,
its carefully placed palms, its endless night.

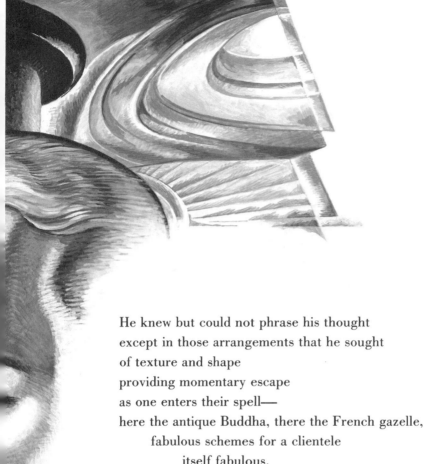

He knew but could not phrase his thought
except in those arrangements that he sought
of texture and shape
providing momentary escape
as one enters their spell—
here the antique Buddha, there the French gazelle,
    fabulous schemes for a clientele
        itself fabulous.
This woman, the Baroness, cannot see
she is now part of my created symmetry.
I have caught her mood;
she is like a marble nude
placed perfectly upon the stairs.
All her aristocratic airs,
her way of talking, her walk, her dress,
will, to visitors, seem fathomless
because of the background I have made,
an arrangement which will ever serenade
    her whim.
As for the Baron, I don't know what to make of him.

So the young man pondered,
feeling he had some part of truth,
that part given to youth, and squandered,
and then made to change—after which—he would rearrange.

"Is it the face of a secret dancing partner you see?"
    asked the Baron, faint mockery
        in his voice as he addressed the Baroness.

"Secret? No, I was thinking of a man who is dead,
        the foreign minister, Herr Rossbach—"

"—a man misled," said the Baron, vehemently.

"—but weren't we all, " the Baroness asked, quietly.

The conversation blends
with a hundred others
seeking other ends
—the murmur of a nightclub crowd
like the wind or sea,
its voice a mystery.

I was an observer of all this,
from my position at the bar,
where I sat eating caviar
and waiting for some woman to appear
in search of a night-wandering cavalier
    such as I,
a man whose manners exemplify
the best one can find at this hour on the avenue.

Jaded? Perhaps, but if you seek a rendezvous,
if you are lonely, bitter, or estranged
I will, for certain advantages exchanged,
provide amusement, cultured conversation, even passion.
In dancing, as in love, I stay with the latest fashion,
    am a skier, mountaineer and sporting man,
    the rugged sort of Bavarian
    with the cool spirit of an Alpine lake,
        in short, a rake,
but one who knows the mountain villages and peaks,
a rogue with whom a woman might spend weeks
before realizing it is she who pays the bill;
the price is exorbitant, but still—
for one who is handsome, strong, and *distingué*,
    is it too much to pay?

I turned, noticing a shadow at the door.
"Come in," said the Waiter, "and join our dancers on the floor."

The Assassin entered,
indifferent to the voices of the night,
sunk in himself, in private candlelight.

I marked him only as one I could ignore,
and returned my gaze to the velvet door
     as it parted again
     revealing the most wretched of men
     an aging queen
     his fat little walk obscene,
        cheeks powdered
        liner on his eyes
    a disguise that is no disguise.

I turned in embarrassment, back to the dance,
    noticing by chance
my own face in the mirror of the bar.
I was smoking, as usual, a thin cigar
but my eyelids had somehow been painted a delicate blue,
    my cheeks tinted another hue
    and my lips the scarlet
    of some effeminate boyish harlot.

I wiped them at once, unsuccessfully,
then heard a voice beside me,
the aging queen smiling at my plight.
"We find ourselves the playthings of the night—"
    He was lighting a cigarette.
"—and unexpectedly we are—the coquette,
    for sleeping beauties rise
in the disguise that is no disguise."

He pointed to the exotic female near us,
      lithe and sensuous
her slender legs coiled round her stool.
"Life is cruel, yet dexterous. That young woman
      is a man. But of course you knew.
      The club has a naked review
      often photographed by the press,
      yet it is anyone's guess
      which gender we have seen
      in the dance incarnadine."

                The conversation blends
                with a hundred others
                seeking other ends . . .

The Headwaiter bowed over a table.
"I'm sorry, we are unable to bring the life Madame ordered.
    Will you accept a substitute?"

. . . and so on, around the room.
The Assassin waits in the gloom
for the hour of his chance.
He does not join the dance.

"My political enemies are many."
    The Baron was filling his glass.
"I watch them pass through oblivion's door
which opens suddenly like the hangman's floor.

"When the evil angel incarnates
he has power, it is true,
but at some point miscalculates
because he is a sick man too,
infantile, unsteady, given to omens.
The Kaiser sought to outdo the Romans
and so it is today.
Politics are a roundelay.
You'll hear the same lines spoken again
by our most prominent citizen.

"And yet you will not hear it as an echo
—the present is difficult to understand.
But those who seize command
are always children somehow given their head.
They will not stop to count the dead . . ."

He does not see me, thought the Baroness,
reaching beneath the table to caress
her pet.

"Miscalculation—" The Baron sipped his anisette.
"—but in the meantime the evil angel, this adolescent boy
      has been given the nation as his toy."

The Baroness's lover nodded at his host
and raised his glass as if to toast
the soliloquy; the Baroness had her hand
      on his knee,
        moved it between his thighs.
The young decorator closed his eyes—*this woman
      is madly indiscreet.*
"Your role in government—" He feigned interest
in the Baron's speech. "—is bittersweet."

"I have uncovered information ruinous to my opponent's career."
The Baron smiled. "His end is near. Our great social climber
      has overestimated the strength of his ledge.
      He will presently be found in the hedge,
        sadly worn, torn to tatters . . ."

None of it, thought the Baroness, *really matters,
men's mad dreams of fame,
it is all, as he says, a child's game.
But he's a child too, he is the same.*

She knew the night's many faces,
knew its doors, halls, staircases,
and dark windows with mournful view.
That alone is our opponent, our lover, our retinue,
but oh my darling, I cling to you
     and you must play your role
     as if you were the living darkness
     that is my soul.

The decorator cast her an embarrassed glance.
I must soon end this romance
before the delicate edges blur
and all that I have made with her
becomes an aging color scheme,
cluttered corners in an expensive dream.

But now the golden tiger crouches
between two snow-white couches
suggesting metaphysical dimension
and the new lamps in ascension
along the mirrored staircase wall
will be hers at nightfall
at the ringing of the evening bell,
made more poignant by my farewell.
It is what the better clientele expect,
a place to weep in and reflect,
above all, a space that is correct.

    The dancers glide on past
    —what affair can last?
    This reflection blends
    with a hundred others,
    seeking other ends.

"Herr Friedlander," asked the barmaid of the powdered little man,
    "how are you tonight?"

"I'm quite well, thank you.
I've made a new friend, you see."
He turned to me
and I turned to the mirror again,
        its most haunted denizen,
        changed to a woman, of sorts.

"We make the least taxing of consorts,"
        Herr Friedlander said quietly.
"We demand little, are sympathetic, droll,
understand the changing nature of the soul,
        its fragile quality,
        its balance on a thread.
I must say, my dear, you look most high-bred;
        good taste and manners are so rare,
        and never have I seen such hair."

My legs were covered in a flowing gown,
I, a man about town, a mountaineer;
how ridiculous I must now appear—
gone my rough good looks and jaunty style,
        exchanged for a painted smile
        and attitude demure.
It was a situation impossible to endure
—and yet I felt a strange freedom in my plight.

"Yes," said Friedlander, "it is characteristic of the night
         that it allows this change
         and allowing it, provides for it
         with a unique range.
You see, you have lost your past.
You are, at last, no one,
for who would claim you as you now are?
What mother, father, or distant star?
A pitiful creature in a dress,
this is the entrance to a wilderness,
         the old rules gone,
         a crooked pathway to the dawn
         which I shall walk with you,
         my darling little ingenue."

What could I do? The night had trapped me
         with a cunning touch.
"Yes, thanks," said Herr Friedlander to the barmaid,
         "thank you so much,"
as she handed him another drink.

I had begun to sink
into feminine thoughts and ways,
a softly-lit and gentle maze.
I suddenly knew the barmaid's heart,
with an intimacy of feeling quite apart
from feelings I'd had before
when I'd considered her more or less a whore—
    now I was a woman too
    and I knew, I knew—
our eyes met and mystery was there,
candlelight reflected in her hair
and sympathy moving between us,
the night itself this flow,
emotions moving to and fro.
I turned toward the Baron's corner of the room,
where his wife's affair put forth its gentle bloom,
the sort of flower one can always see
    despite attempts at secrecy.

The Baron knew he was deceived by love.
"The hand of night, a woman, wears a black glove
        to hide her marriage to a friend."
He knew that even ancient love must end
        —thus, what of the human sort?
I've wasted myself, he thought, at the Chancellor's court.
        He was remembering the Baroness, how she'd been
        when they were young and he her paladin
                rising to the dance.

"We cannot trust our heart to chance,"
        he added, looking in her eyes,
and then at her companion, a young man easy to despise,
who, he was certain, would soon be gone
leaving her older than the mastodon,
and dry as a moth's cocoon,
this young comet who laughs at the aging moon.

"Well," said the young man, "chance is all we know.
It has brought me designs that seem to grow
        into what may have been my plan.
But I do not deceive myself, I am one who understands
        we are helpless before our fate . . ."

Yes, thought the Baron, a young man easy to hate,
        with the assurance of the fool.
How grotesque to find myself his tool
        and suffer his insolence tonight,
but such are the ways of the parasite . . .

The Baroness saw only her lover's antique grace,
something of the minstrel in his face,
one, in any case, who lives on fashion's edge.
Clad in velvet, he moves me toward the ledge
    of which my husband speaks.
    I haven't been myself for weeks.
    I've fallen, or will fall,
    helpless and beyond recall.

"But," she said, "the night is attracted to the dawn,
    who is youthful, and some say a swan,
seductive, luring night ever from her cave."
    She looked at him. "Or is dawn a knave?"

The decorator laughed. "We are enjoying ourselves, I think—"
    This woman has had too much to drink
    and seeks to make a scene.
    Why can't she be content with what has been,
    with memories of a tasteful interlude.
    But no, she wishes to be crude . . .

The Waiter came, bearing the tray of night,
clear glass, with inscribed moons and incidental light.
    "Madame's ambrosia, with lemon rind—
    and for the gentlemen, a mixture undefined,
    secret, known only to Berlin
    but in its depths a dancing djinn.

    "So now, I am at your service, the night has far to go
    and the human soul is an embryo."

"What did he mean by that?" asked the Baroness.
Beneath the table she passed a caress
as she opened her evening purse.
This affair, she thought, has turned for worse;
my young man, remote and bored,
after having made me feel adored,
is cruel, like a beautiful bird,
and I am foolish, my position absurd.

She touched a drop of scent to her neck,
nervously, as if somehow to check
the disintegration of the hour she had known
—but the hour is not held by application of cologne.

"Our waiter," said the Baron, "is an observer here.
    "His commentary is remarkably clear,
    and he is right, we sleep inside a womb,
    at the moment, this room.
    Who of us has yet been born?
    How many have seen the unicorn?"

    The conversation blends
    with a hundred others
    seeking other ends . . .

The Assassin was passing the club's bare stage,
proscenium and apron trimmed with artificial foliage
which, when lit would frame the chorus in hanging bowers,
     paper flowers on wire stems
     to match the cardboard diadems
in the revue dedicated to Queen Venus.

Past love's arbor, the predator stalked, and moved between us,
     Herr Friedlander and I making room
     for this messenger of the tomb.

Herr Friedlander smiled and called the barmaid near.
"Please, a drink for this fellow here . . ."

The Assassin turned toward Friedlander then,
wondering what sort of little hen
he had to deal with until the moment came,
when he would rise and take slow aim . . .

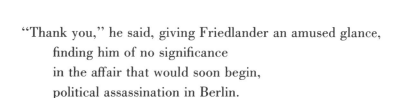

"Thank you," he said, giving Friedlander an amused glance,
    finding him of no significance
    in the affair that would soon begin,
    political assassination in Berlin.

"It is my pleasure," Friedlander said,
"for I see you are acquainted with the dead—"

The Assassin went very still,
a sudden silence that was his skill,
and I felt the presence of another at his side,
    invisible, ancient, and dignified
from whom the Assassin took strength and breath.

"And you," the Assassin smiled, "you know of Death?"

"I know the shape of night and what it has designed."
Friedlander seemed now not nearly so inclined
to proceed in conversation, and edged away.
"Excuse me, I am just an old habitué,
and my games are foolish, often rude.
Forgive me, I did not mean to intrude—"
He seemed to bow, not to the Assassin
but to the spectre at the Assassin's shoulder,
as if to one who was a great deal older,
    who knew all, habitué and whore,
who would touch us but once and then no more.

Friedlander mingled with the dancers, disappeared,
    and, as I had feared,
      the Assassin turned to me.
I met his glance, elusively,
but his eyes held no reflection of my face.
He seemed to stare through an empty space.

I turned toward the mirror's dark blue glass
but no trace of my face there passed,
only a wisp of smoke from my cigarette,
slowly becoming a woman's silhouette,
her arm extended, her manner shy,
eyes glowing faintly as a firefly.

Her hair, smoke-colored, smoke-shaped
fell upon her shoulders and escaped
down her back in trailing wisps of silver-gray—
this creature, a sort of drifting Salome,
    was what I had become
to the turning of the dancers and the beating of the drum.

"These hours," said the Baron to his wife,
"may be all we have left of life . . ."
What thoughts are these, he wondered silently.
Do I defend against her infidelity?

He wanted to invoke their happy past,
but knew he'd turn to brutality and bombast,
give a lecture, address the government,
be forceful, filled with logic, even eloquent,
but lacking the simple feeling of their youth
when the slightest gesture held their truth.
I am paralyzed by what I have become,
to the turning of the dancers and the beating of the drum.

The Baroness saw her husband through a veil,
could not discern that he had grown pale,
weighed down by something in the room.
She was closing her tiny bottle of perfume
as a memory came to her,
reminding her of how they were—
he in a straw hat and she, a parasol on her arm,
a faded memory filled with charm.
Yes, there was a small country inn,
a sitting room where so many things begin—
sunlight falling across the floor,
the innkeeper's footstep in the corridor
bringing us coffee, a slice of cake, some fruit.
     If only memory were mute
but no, it has my husband's voice,
and so, my eyes are moist,
and I recall the singing of small caged birds
    by the window, and his words
    were mignonettes.
Is this my hour for regrets?
"I am remembering just now—"

A length of veil had been taken from her brow,
but her young man, through some slight spur
resumed his attentions to her,
and she fell back into his net,
forgetting the past and the green-white mignonette.

"I think we must do the downstairs hall."
He smiled. "We must not neglect it, after all . . ."
His hand grazed hers beneath the table.
"We must find a Chinese vase, large and stable,
and in the shadows something small, a statuette . . ."
No, I mustn't abandon her just yet,
for commissions of this sort are rare,
and really, I've been working with a flair,
        her house my masterpiece.
It would be self-indulgent were I to cease
just because her lips no longer fascinate.

". . . and at the hallway's end, a gate,
suggesting an infinite expanse . . ."
He smiled again. "I must be inspired by the dance."

The conversation blends
with a hundred others,
seeking other ends . . .

The Waiter paused before my smoke-like shape.
"Madame will be interested in this, the subtle grape."
He handed me a glass filled with mist.
"From the vine of dreams the moon has kissed . . ."

He withdrew through pillars where night-flowers hung,
leaving the cloud-drink upon my tongue.
I swallowed.
Understanding followed,
and I turned back toward the bar.
Seated there, smoking his cigar,
was the man I'd been when night first fell,
    gigolo, dull sentinel
watching for some opportunity, some chance
to improve his position in the dance.

And I was his unknown soul,
beyond his reason and control
—an unseen partner in that dance
he performed with such arrogance.

I knew the secret of this room,
that it was a dream agreed upon, heirloom
of the dream that had preceded it
in a series that was infinite
and all the dancers infinite too
dancing ever and endlessly through
  the smoke
until, by some magic in their turning, they awoke
to find they were nothing more than atmosphere,
  candleflames dancing in a chandelier.
  They too were dreams,
deceptive as the artificial moonbeams
cast by the dance floor's incandescent spot.
  They were, and they were not.
Their lithe forms of feline grace
were vacant mirrors adrift in space;
like phantasms born of opium
they floated, insubstantial, to the beating of the drum.

"Escape now, young lady," said the Waiter, returning to my side,
    "for the revelation has a tendency to hide
      and you may find yourself enslaved once more
      within that gentleman seated by the dance floor."

He pointed to my corporal form, the professional rake
    who'd still be at the bar come daybreak,
      bragging softly, lost in games,
      collecting women, dropping names.
"I can't foresee," I said, "return to such a state."

"Between reality and dream we vacillate."

"You who see so much," I asked, "why do you remain?"

"I have a fondness for champagne,"
he said, exploding a cork past my eyes.
I watched the spirit from the bottle rise,
    gay, golden grapes in her hair,
    laughing and swirling through the air,
    a creature more scintillating than any at the bar,
    at her throat a ruby star
    to show that part of us she rules,
Champagne, goddess of fools.

But—the Assassin drank no gay wine,
or if he drank he gave no sign
that lightness of heart might stay his hand
or lead him to join the dancer's saraband.
He moved now, through the tables, up the aisle,
    upon his face a frozen smile
and behind him, Death, in spectral hood.

The Baron saw and understood.

He drew the pocket-pistol he always wore
and tipped the table to the floor.
The Baroness felt his arm, sudden steel,
forcing her to kneel
behind the makeshift barricade.

The Assassin fired his fusillade,
motion having slowed for him,
figures moving as if they sought to swim
in some thick substance of the dream,
on their lips the beginning of a scream,
as each one pierced the moment to its core,
and Death the only dancer on the floor.

Of the other figures one moved swifter than the rest,
with the calm of the self-possessed,
in the same attitude of grace Death wore.
Herr Friedlander, unlikely matador,
between the Assassin and his prey
stepped with the step of the habitué
who knows the club, its every mood,
and chooses this moment to conclude
    his quest,
the Assassin's bullets in his chest,
and one of the Baron's in his back,
Friedlander collecting each thundercrack,
his body twitching in the roar,
then falling gently to the floor,
as the Assassin withdrew through the crowd,
followed by a shadow in a shroud.

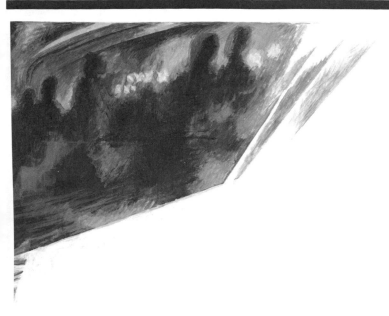

I found myself at Friedlander's side
and felt the outward flowing of the tide
that had been his days and nights,
his secret storehouse and his plights.
His eyes were mirrors of Berlin,
all that he had known and been
     surfacing in one last glance.

"If you seek . . . the meaning of romance . . ."
He gasped, and moved his hand,
trying to help me understand
what he knew now, of the dancing floor,
at the opening of the night's most inner door,
but his voice had become a whisper and a sigh,
and I heard only the Baron behind me, asking "Why?
     Why did he become my shield?"

Friedlander smiled, and nodded, as if he had revealed
     the answer to the riddle of the human soul,
       its origin, its fabric, and its goal.

I heard a woman far away
imploring me to remember what I'd heard Friedlander say
and I saw my form was masculine again.
I'd rejoined the world of men,
was again the gigolo.
What had Friedlander said? I did not know.
The woman of smoke had heard Friedlander's whispered answer
but I was just a ballroom dancer,
reflected in the polished wood.
I had not understood
and Friedlander now was dead.

There was no more dancing nor beating of the drum,
and yet I heard music. Or was it delirium?
There seemed to be an aspect of the dance
subject neither to time nor chance,
but continuing always, above the room,
in its mirrors, within its gloom,
where invisible dancers continued their round.
     Perfectly free? Or hopelessly bound?

I stood, the Baron at my side.
"That he, in my place, should have died—"
The Baron's face was filled with remorse,
but the Waiter replied, "There was no other course,
    it was the design of fate."

"We say such things when it is too late."
The Baron knelt and whispered in Friedlander's ear.
Perhaps—who knows—the dead can hear.

The conversation blends
with a hundred others,
seeking other ends . . .

The Baroness was trembling with a match,
something within her beginning to detach,
as if she'd found a place entirely her own,
a place whose existence she hadn't known,
    free from illusions of the heart,
    where one no longer plays a part,
    nor finds the need to rearrange,
    a place free from the insistent voice of change.

It was in that little man's eyes, she thought
    and can neither be seduced nor bought.
    His final glance imparted it to me,
    indeterminate, all shadowy . . .

"Are you alright?" Her young man was getting to his feet,
    and she saw each facet of his deceit,
    his calculating charm, his greed,
and she wondered how he'd ever filled her need,
which was answered only by this uncertain place,
    this feeling in her, this veiled face,
no more definite than a street corner in the rain
    to which I will find my way again,
    footsteps echoing in the dark,
    along the avenue and then through the park . . .

"I think our evening has ended," said the young man.
  "You will not be offended if—"
He was gathering up his cloak, his gloves,
and he would have to gather other loves,
for this woman's clearly enough was through.
It's odd, he thought, what a few gunshots will do.
He stepped past Friedlander, gave the police his name,
    thinking that it truly was a shame
    the Baroness's downstairs hall must go undone,
    or be done by just anyone,
      for in a day or two, he was quite sure,
when her afternoon becomes impossible to endure,
she'll be looking for a designer's company,
but I'm certain, quite certain, it won't be me.

"Good night, sir," said the Waiter at the door.
"We're sorry, and hope to host you and your party once more . . ."

"Not likely," said the decorator.

The conversation blends . . .

I, the ladies' man, was leaving too,
with other avenues to pursue,
other clubs along the way
that I would travel to the day.

Of course I'd not been left untouched,
but it does not do to dwell too much
on such experiences as I'd just had,
of Friedlander's death and myself so oddly clad,
 in a woman's form, smoke-ringed, strange.
Such thoughts could easily derange
 a sensitive observer of the night.

Ahead was the city square, bathed in moonlight,
and a lone figure stood beneath the lamppost's glow.
It turned toward me, its movements slow,
 dreamlike, like a dancer's.

My mind recoiled, afraid of answers
that would force it to the brink.
It was Friedlander, or so I could only think,
for the face was his, and the rotund shape,
but behind him the street had become a landscape
 from some other world
into which I felt I would be hurled
if I took another step toward him there,
upon that transcendental city square.

". . . if you seek . . . the meaning of romance . . ."

Within the landscape, then, I saw the dance
of creatures whose sex was impossible to know,
beautiful beings, feathered, jeweled, upon some plateau
of feelings so complex and rare
that to gaze at them was to be aware
that we have only just begun to dance.

". . . seek . . . the meaning of romance . . ."

Friedlander's form was joining theirs,
as if he were moving up a flight of stairs,
and as he climbed he became adorned,
    moon-crowned, horned,
a royal shape of an ancient god,
the little man I'd thought so odd,
now a deity of the moon-ruled clan,
that laughable little half-a-man,
majestic, a leader of the dance,
powerful, beautiful, the soul of romance.

"Friedlander," I cried, "take me too!"

But he was fading with his retinue,
fading into the perfect dark,
into the inner regions of the city park.

I stood alone. Masculine? Feminine?
This is—seduction in Berlin.